DECORATIVE TILE DESIGNS
in Full Color

Selected and Arranged by

CAROL BELANGER GRAFTON

DOVER PUBLICATIONS, INC.
New York

Copyright © 1992 by Dover Publications, Inc.
All rights reserved under Pan American and International
Copyright Conventions.

Published in Canada by General Publishing Company, Ltd.,
30 Lesmill Road, Don Mills, Toronto, Ontario.

Decorative Tile Designs in Full Color
is a new work, first published by Dover Publications, Inc., in 1992.
See the Publisher's Note for the sources of the plates.

DOVER *Pictorial Archive* SERIES

Manufactured in the United States of America
Dover Publications, Inc.
31 East 2nd Street
Mineola, N.Y. 11501

Library of Congress Cataloging-in-Publication Data

Grafton, Carol Belanger.
Decorative tile designs in full color / selected and arranged by
Carol Belanger Grafton.
p.   cm. — (Dover pictorial archive series)
ISBN 0-486-26952-3
1. Tiles—Themes, motives.   I. Title.   II. Series.
NK4670.G73   1992
745.4—dc20   91-32306
CIP

PUBLISHER'S NOTE

 The grand style of public, palatial and ecclesiastical architecture has long entailed the use of decorative floor and wall tiling, which still today strikingly enhances the effects of splendor and permanence integral to the architectural conception.

Decorative tiles were first used in the Middle East some 4000 years ago, and gradually spread throughout the region and to the southern Mediterranean. They seem to have appeared in Europe only early in the current millennium (centuries after the arrival of mosaic), when they reached Spain via the Moors.

The principles of Islamic design have tended to prevail ever since. The motifs are generally abstract (reflecting a religious tradition prohibiting artistic representation of living things), though floriated and foliated designs are also numerous; and a mass of detail usually fills in all the available area, without creating a strongly "hierarchical" structure—a highly practical principle that permits considerable adaptation in the design's overall proportions.

The patterns on the following pages have been selected from catalogs published between about 1870 and 1930 by two English manufacturers, Maw & Co. of Broseley, Shropshire, and Campbell Tile Co. of Stoke-upon-Trent; two Spanish firms, Gabarró, Tarrida y Compª of Igualada and E. F. Escofet y Cª of Barcelona; and two French firms, E. Thomazeau of Cérizay (Deux-Sèvres) and Marquet Frères of Andrézieux (Loire); plus a collection by the French artist A. Cheneveau and published by the Maison F. Delarue & Fils, Paris. Many of the designs are credited, several to artists and architects of some reputation in their time. They appear, of course, greatly reduced, reflecting ratios of 1:6, 1:8, 1:10, 1:15 and 1:16.

In the original catalogs the tiles are recommended for use in a variety of buildings (schools, churches, conservatories, public buildings) and areas (courtyards, halls, vestry rooms, lobbies, vestibules) and for numerous specific surfaces and purposes (fireplaces, pilasters, furniture, flowerboxes, stringcourses, dadoes, friezes, moldings, altar rails and steps, ecclesiastical pavements, inscriptions, baths, skirtings, fenders). The hearth designs can be recognized by their shape (see pp. 52, 53, 58 and 66). The many strip patterns are obviously appropriate for moldings, stringcourses and the like. And the basic bordered "carpet" format could, for most designs, readily be adapted to broader rectangular floor and wall surfaces of many differing proportions.

In these 416 examples the designer and architect of the present day will rediscover the dazzling richness of a great tradition.

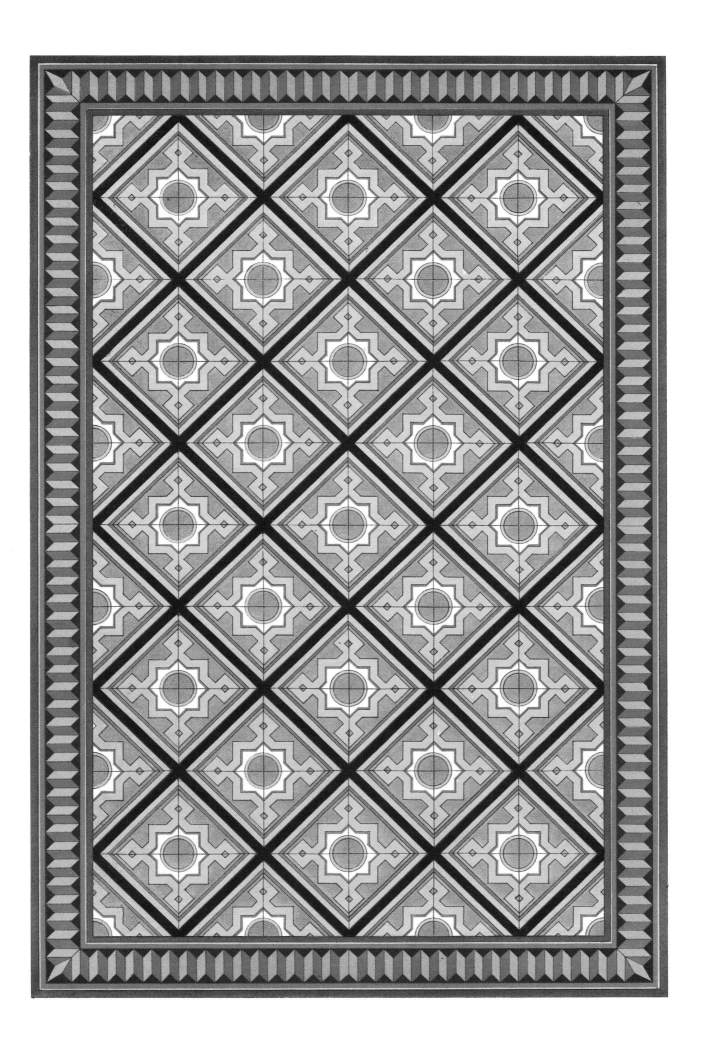

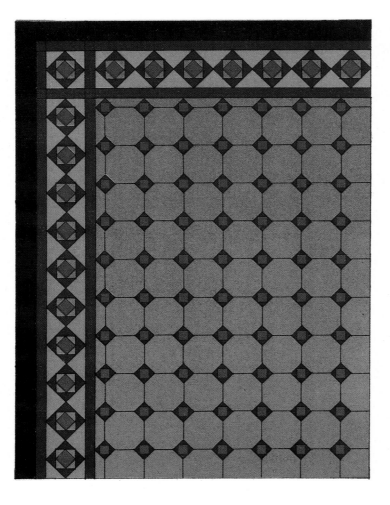

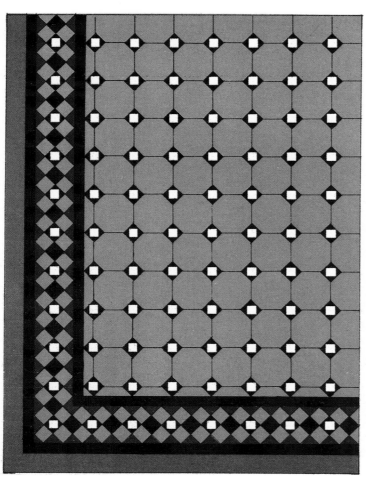
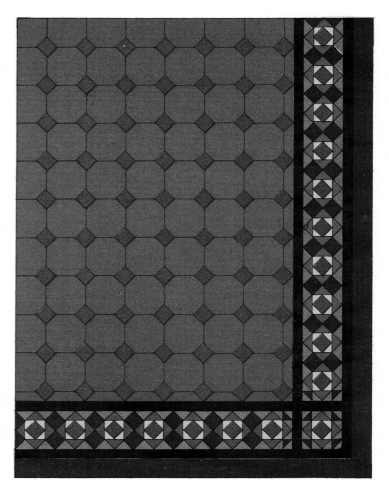

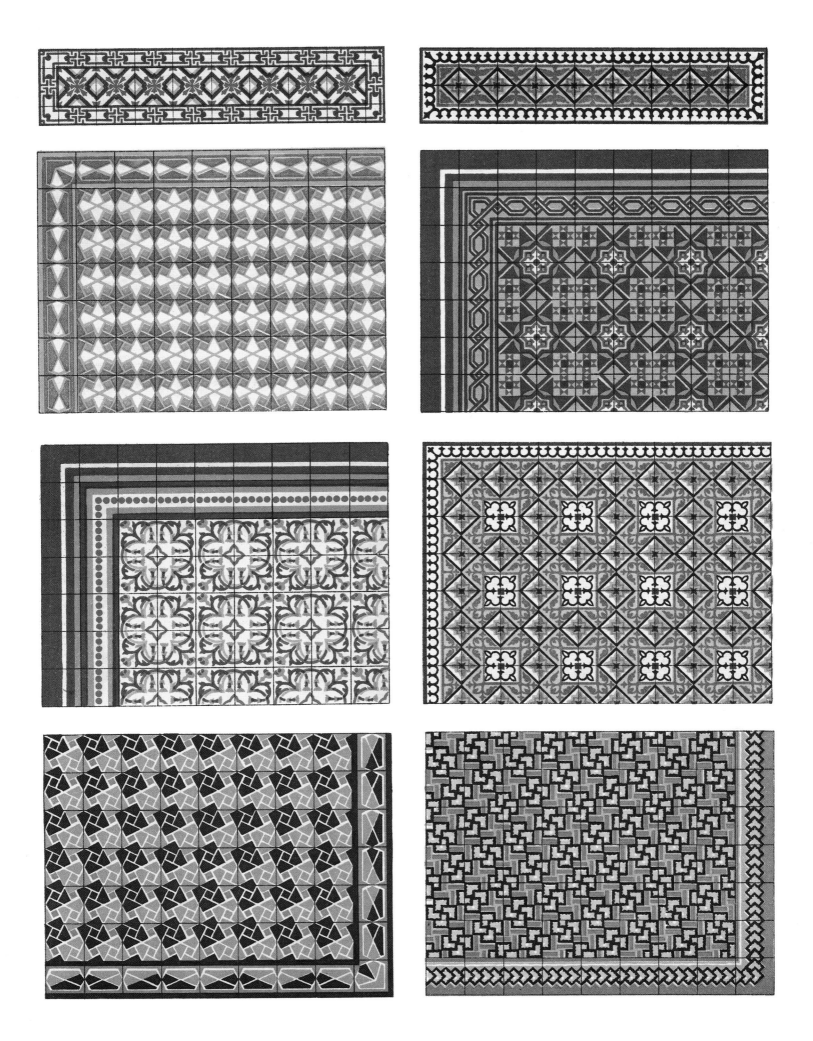

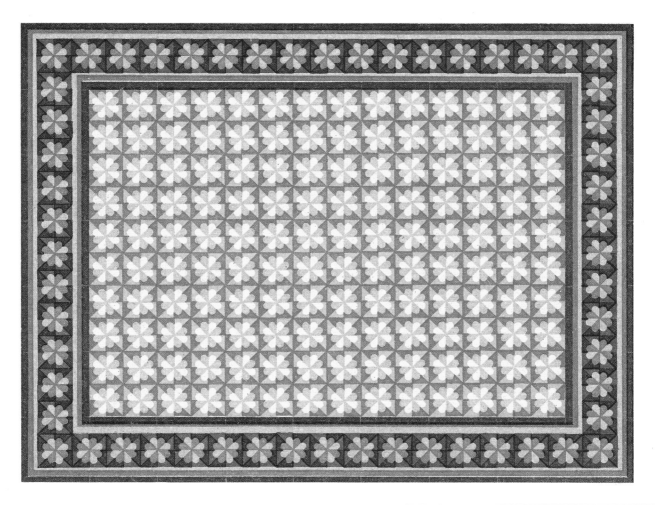

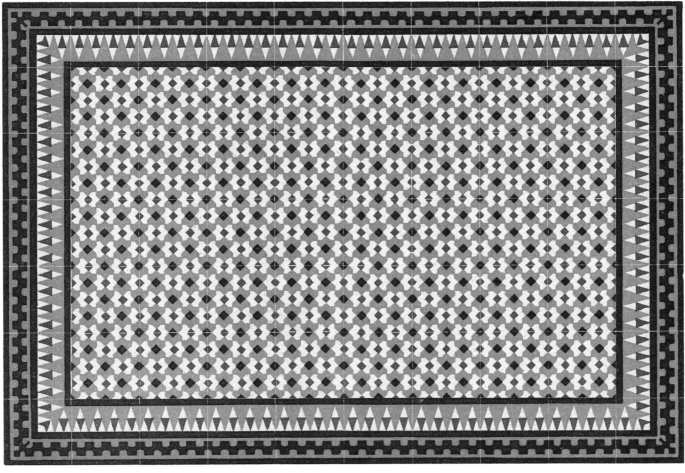

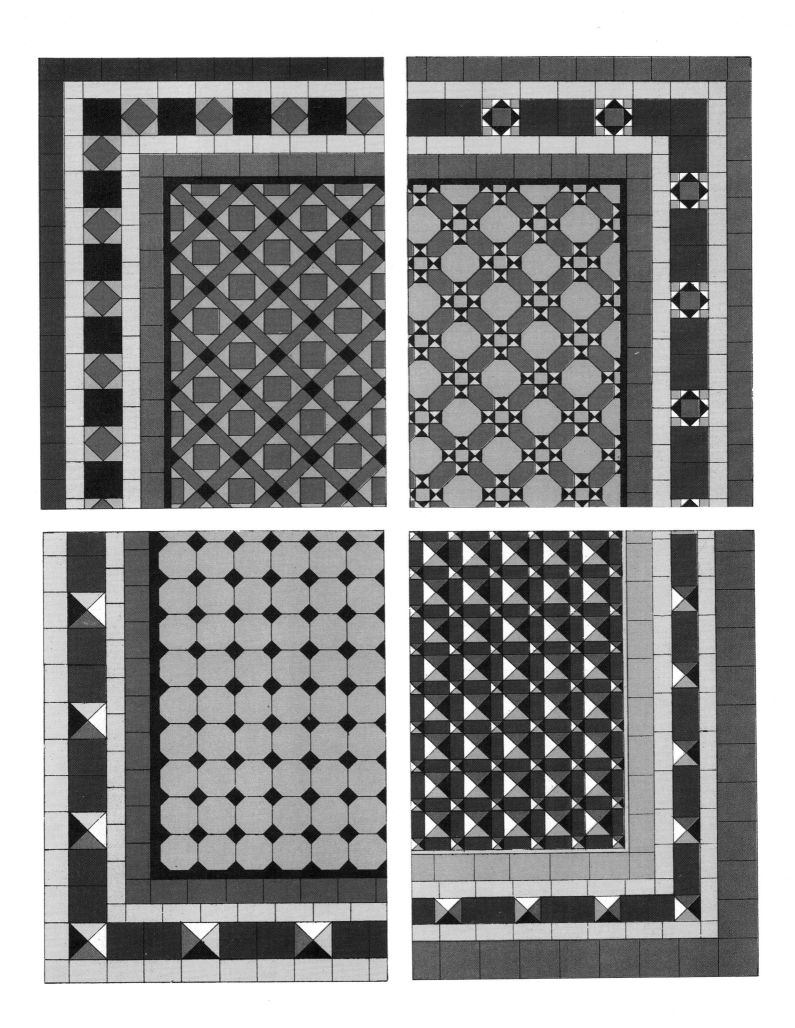

13

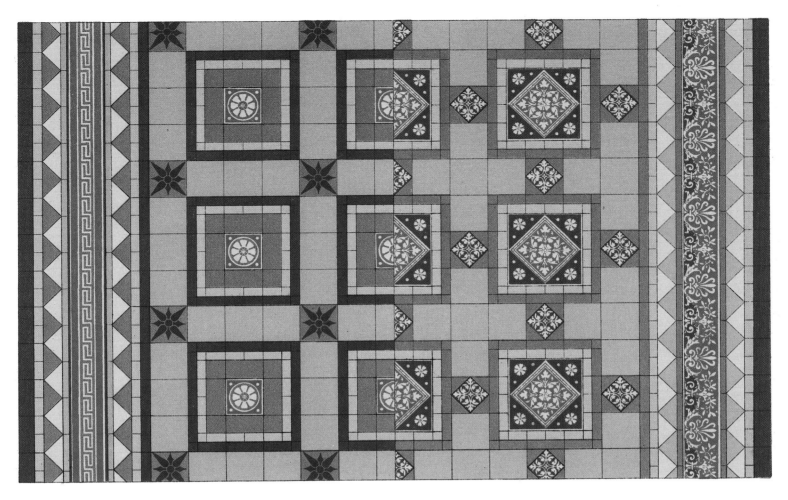

17

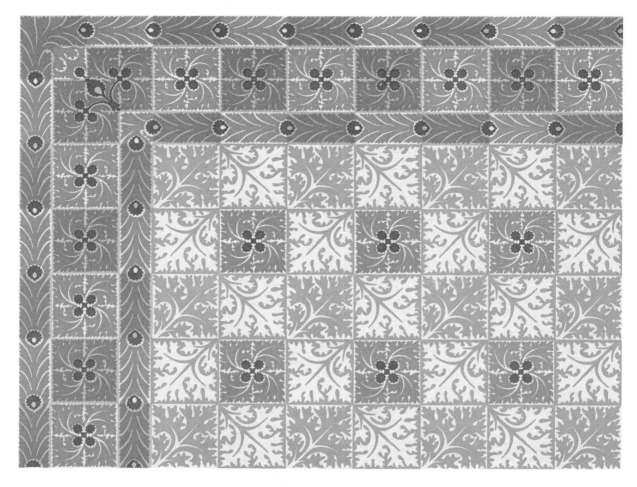

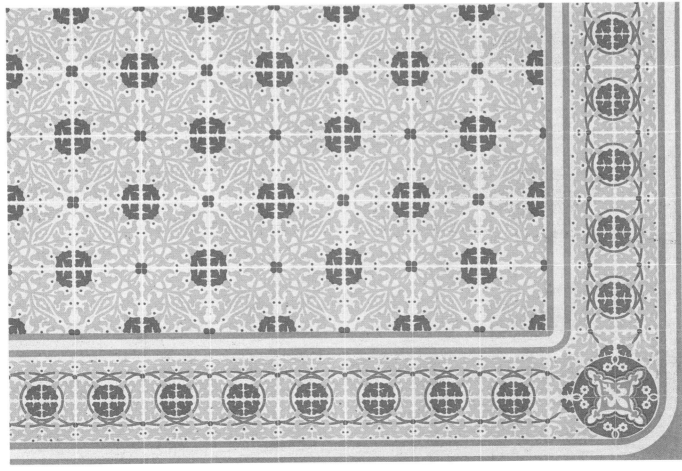

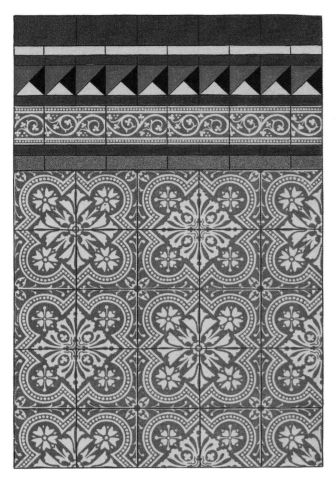

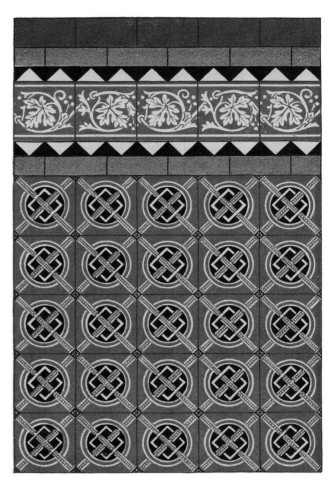

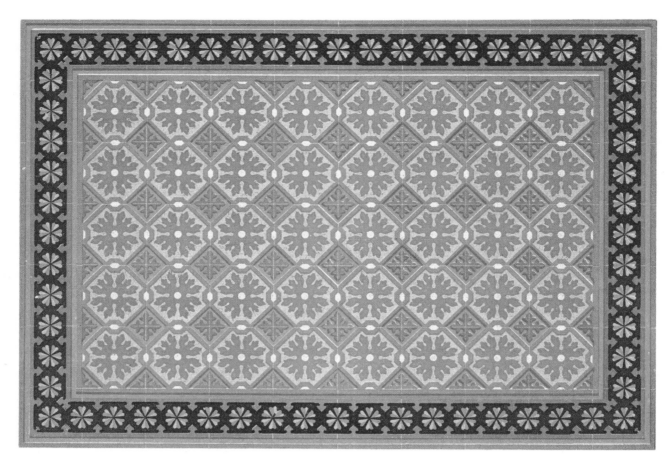

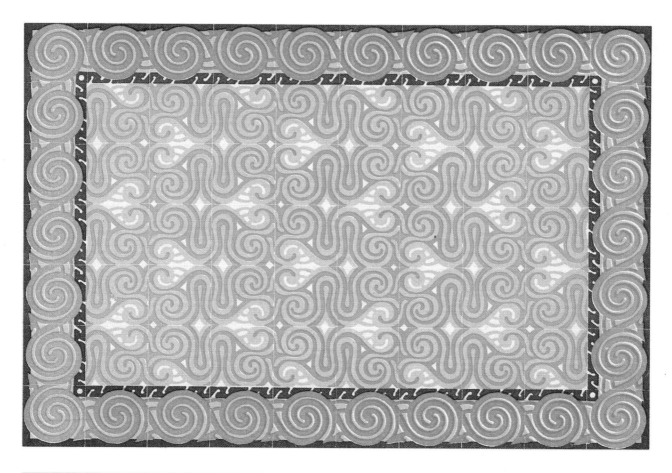

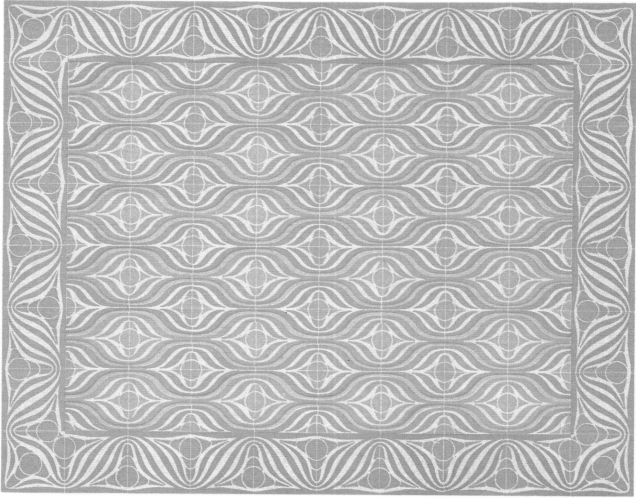

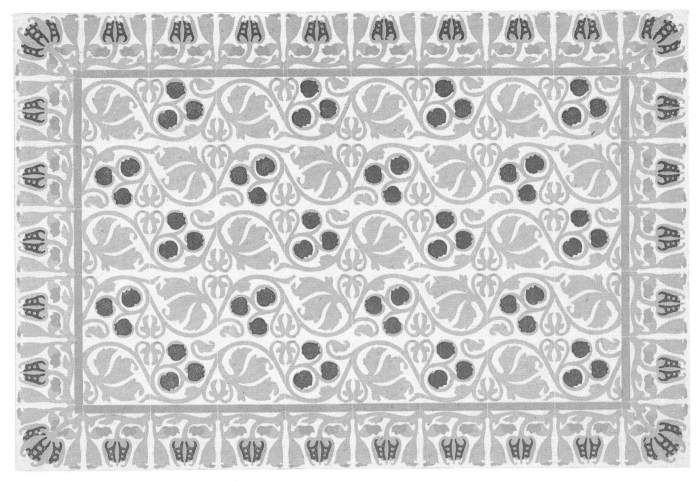

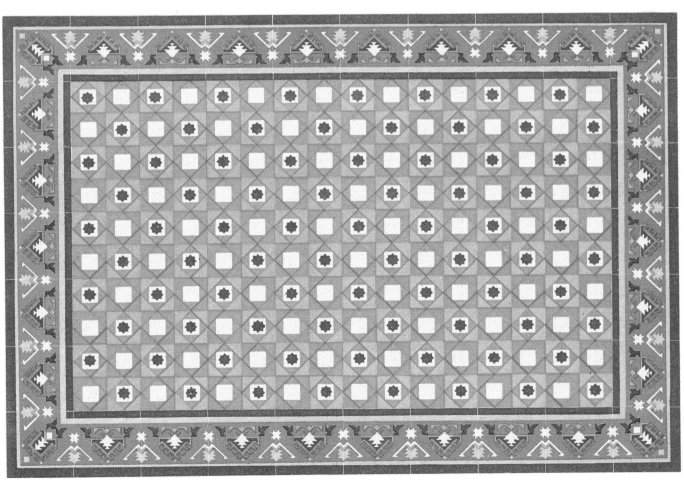

27

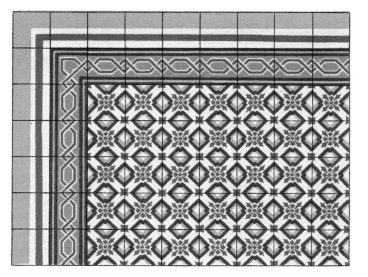

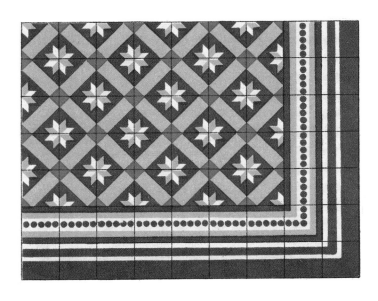

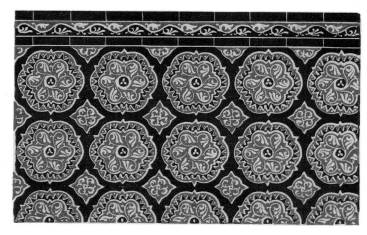

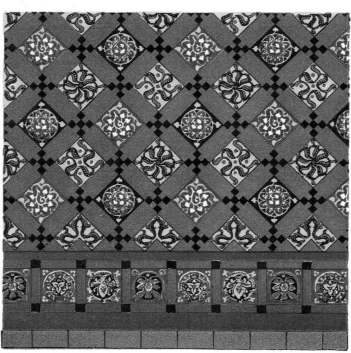
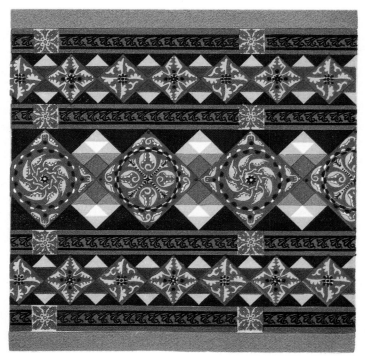

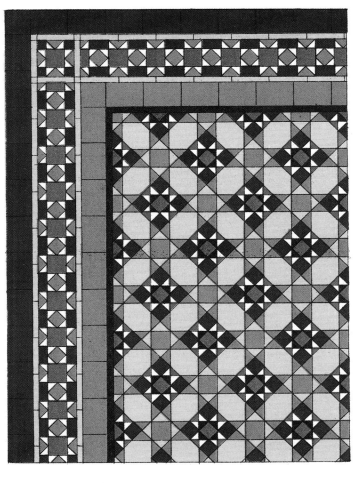

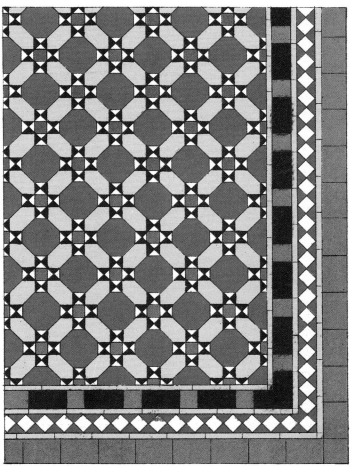

33

34

38

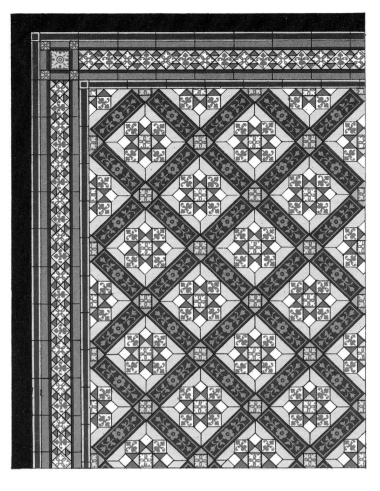

39

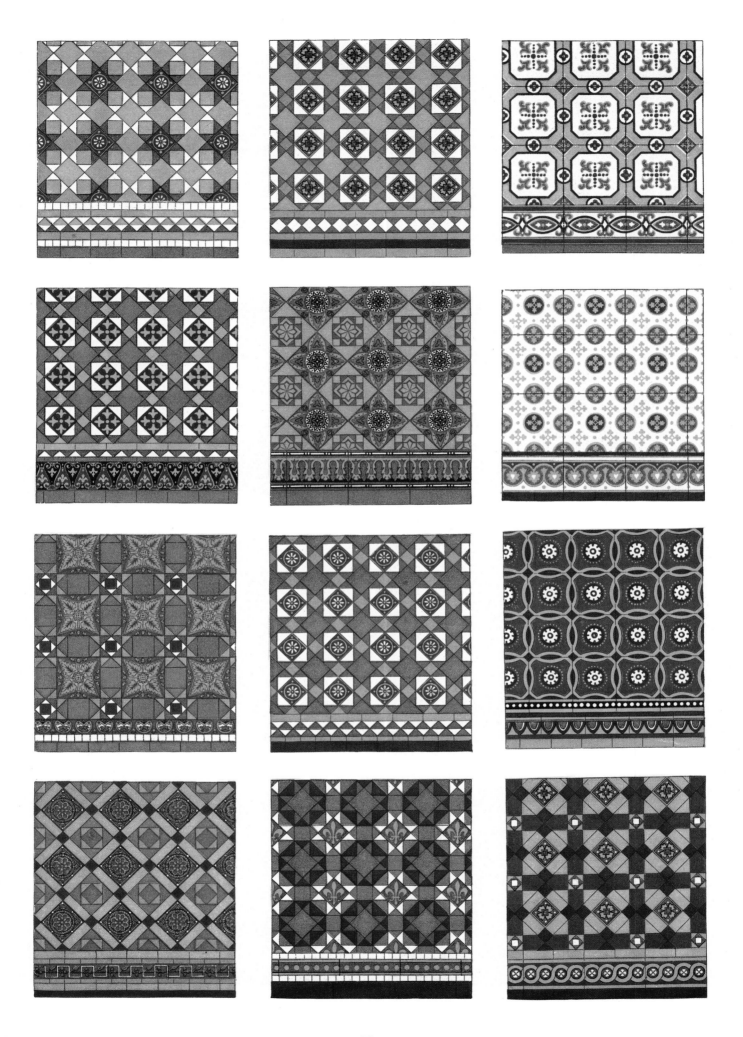

40

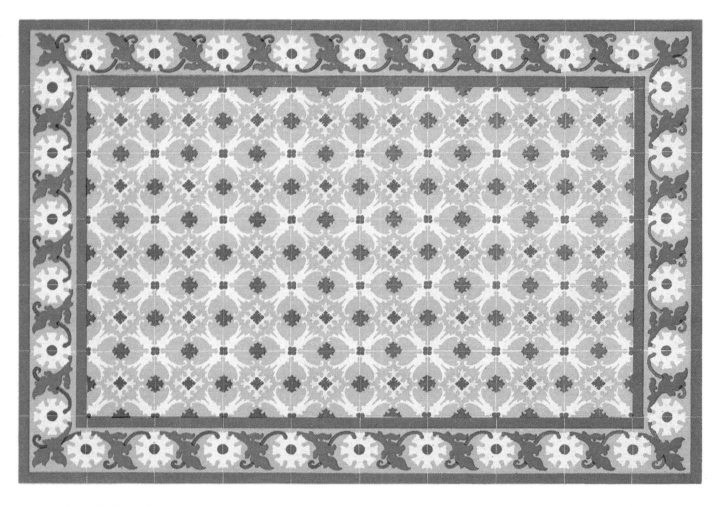

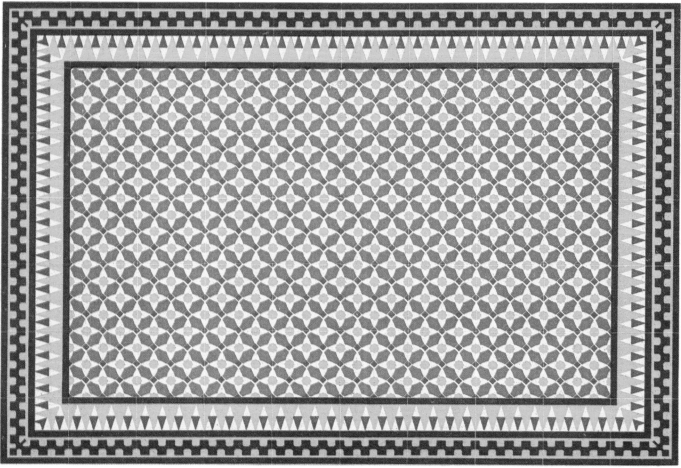

44

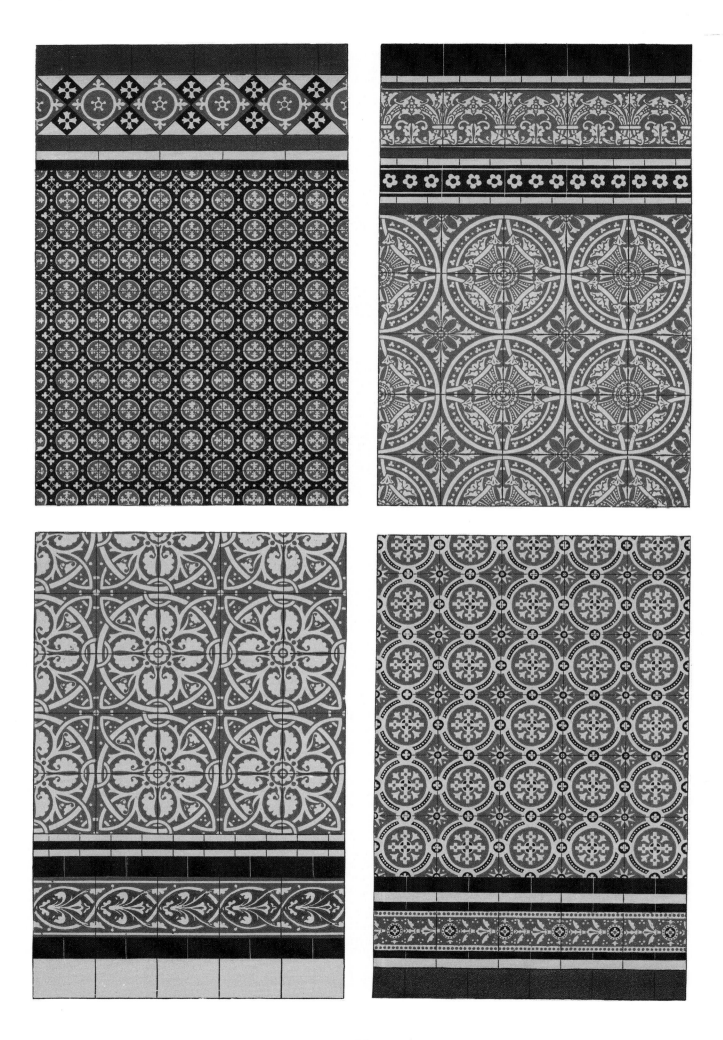

47

48

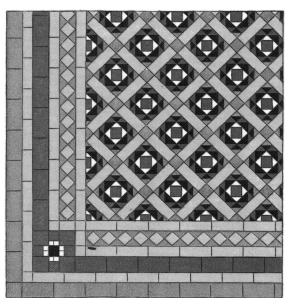

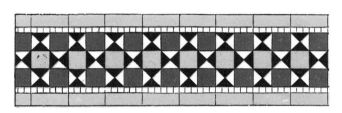

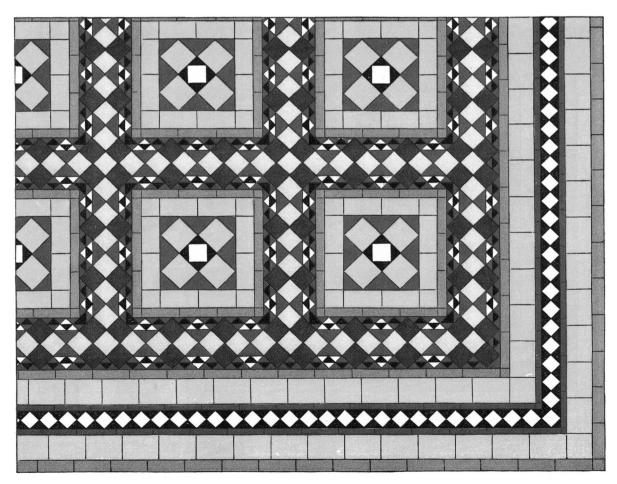

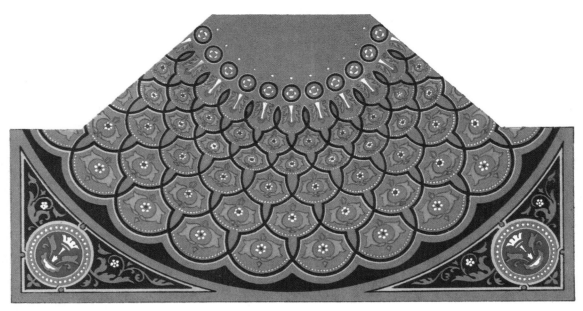

53

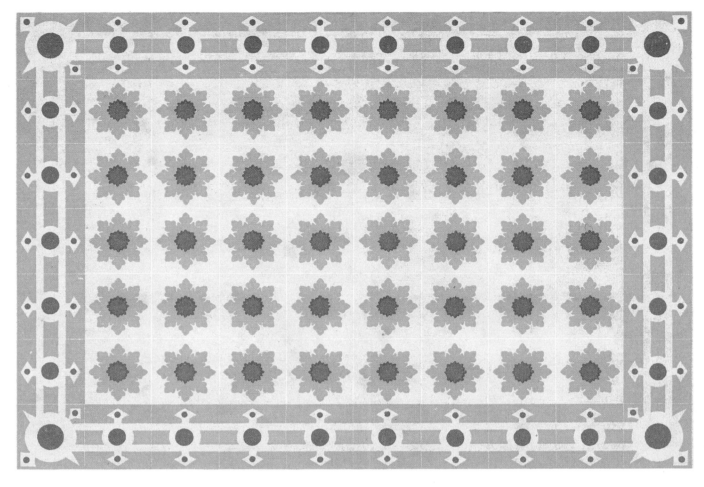

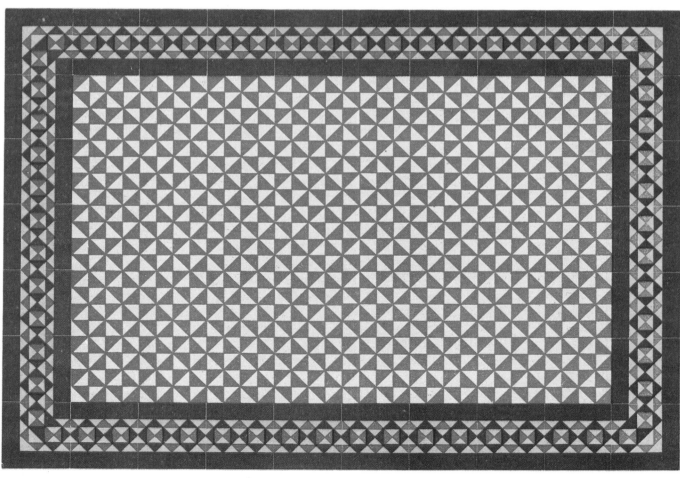

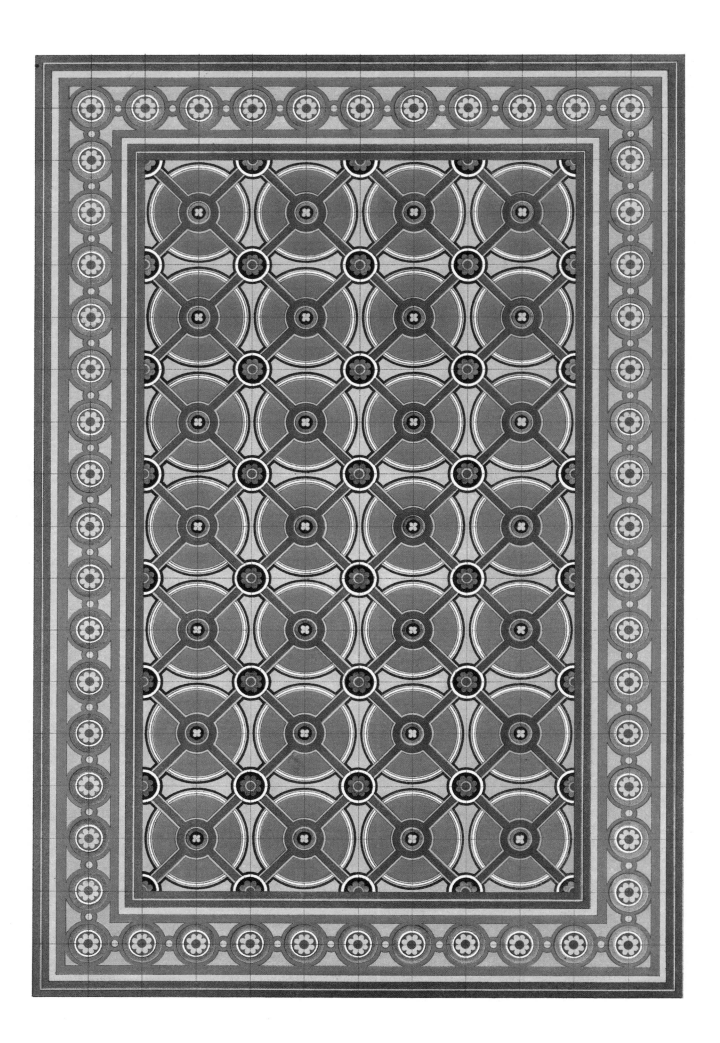

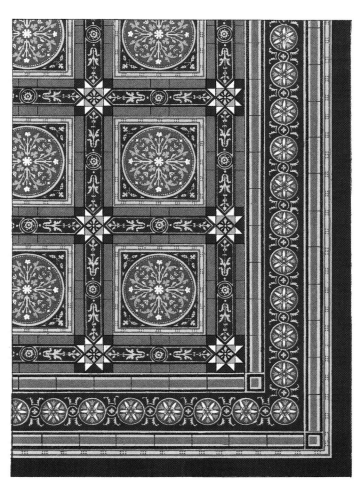

57

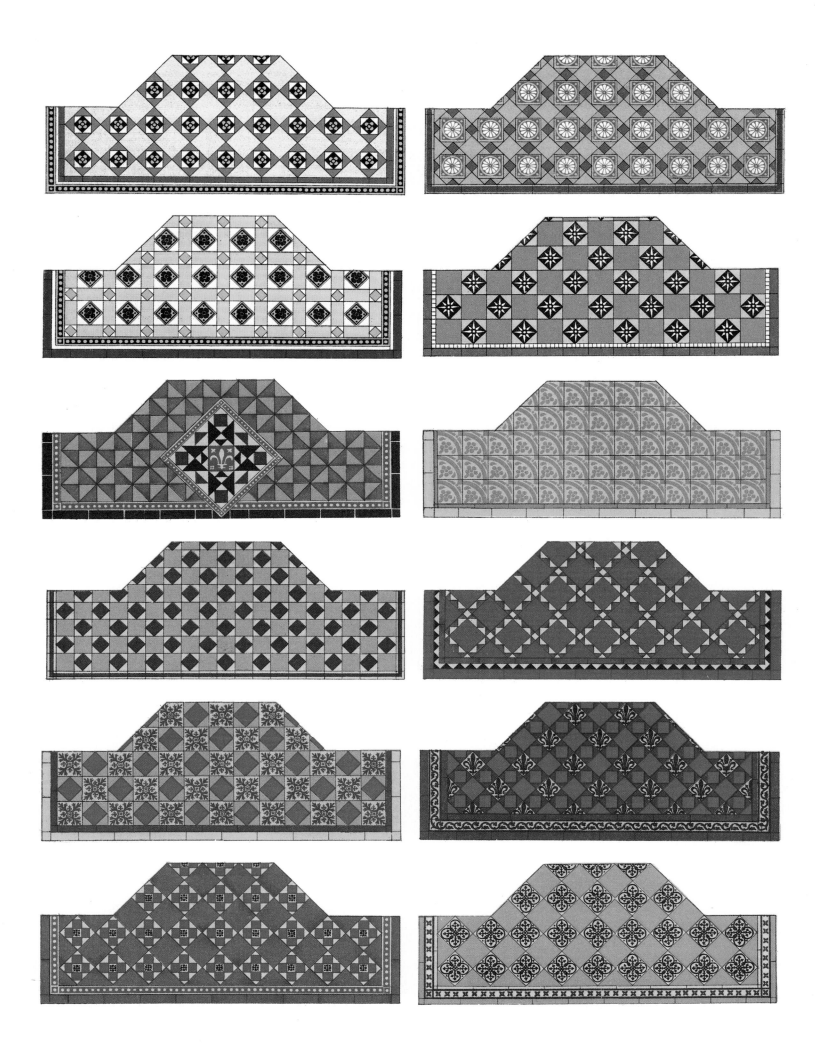

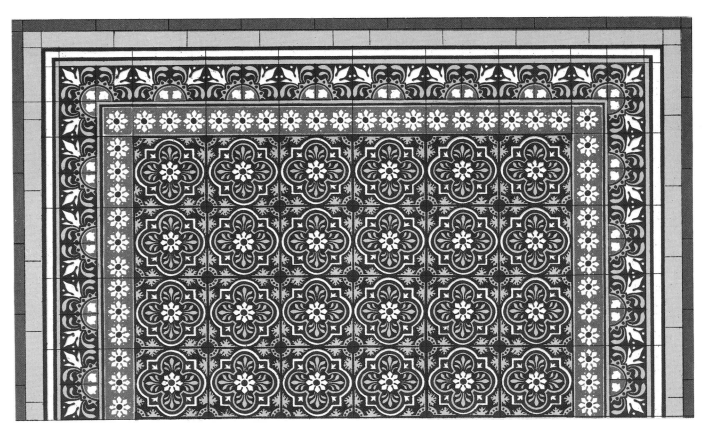

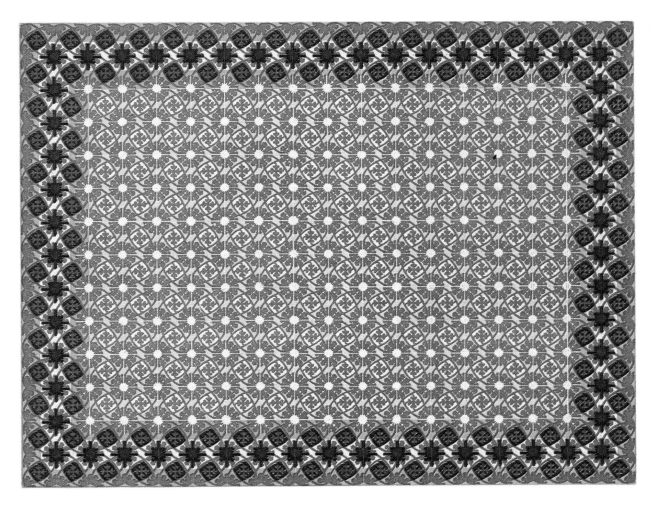

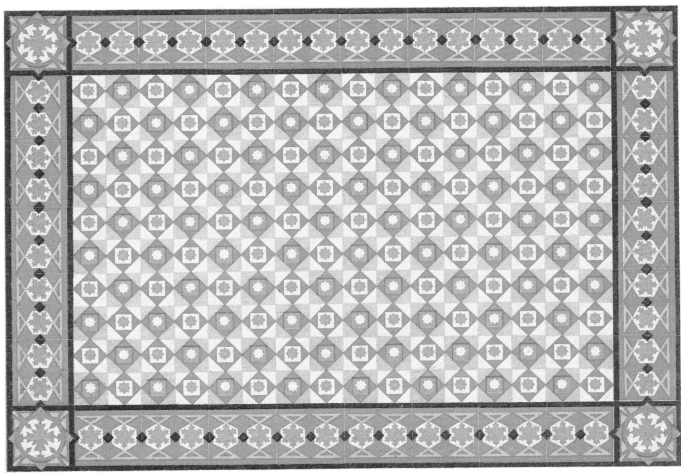

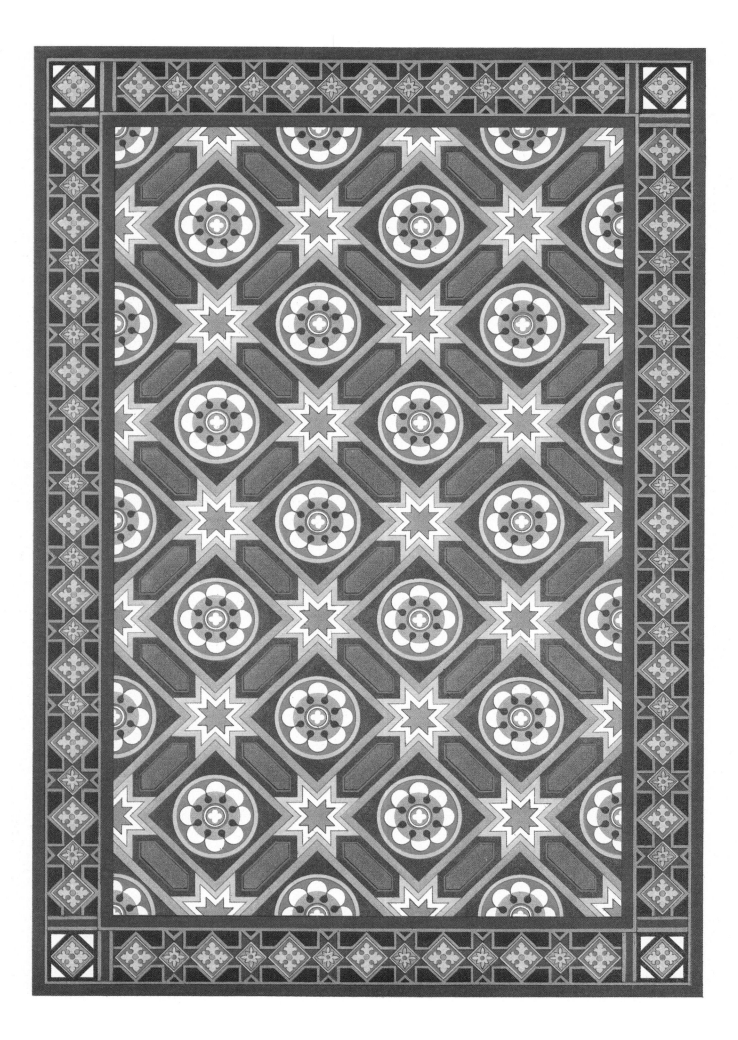

65

66

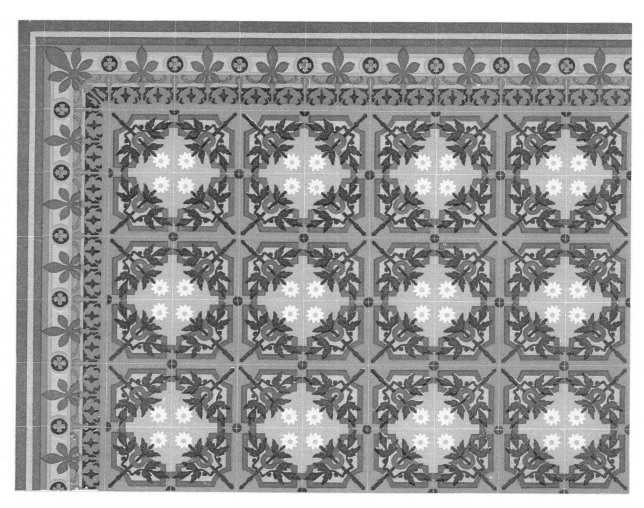

68

69

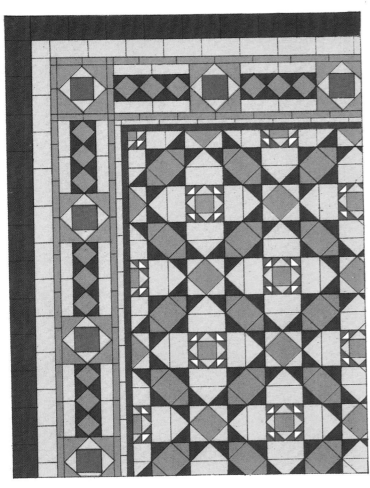

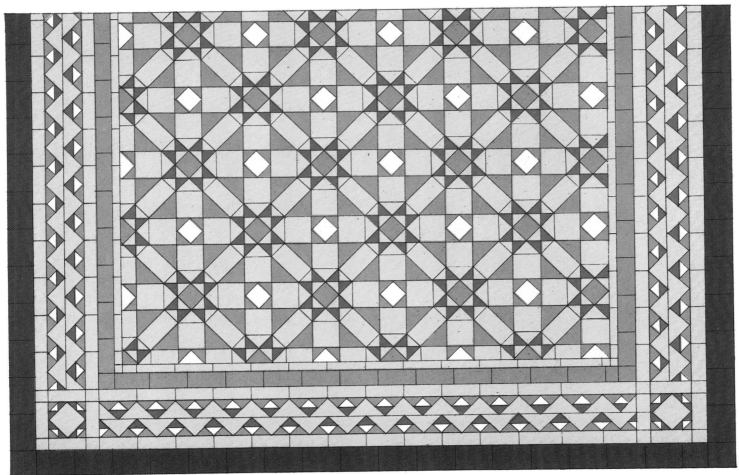

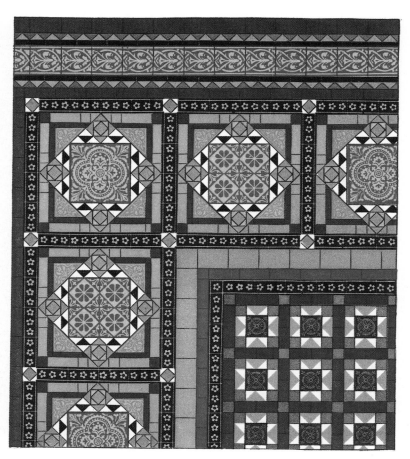

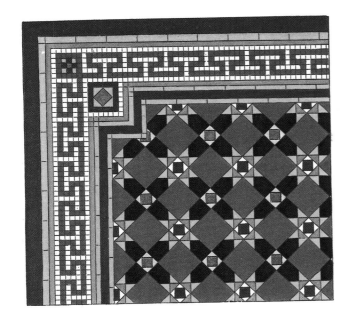

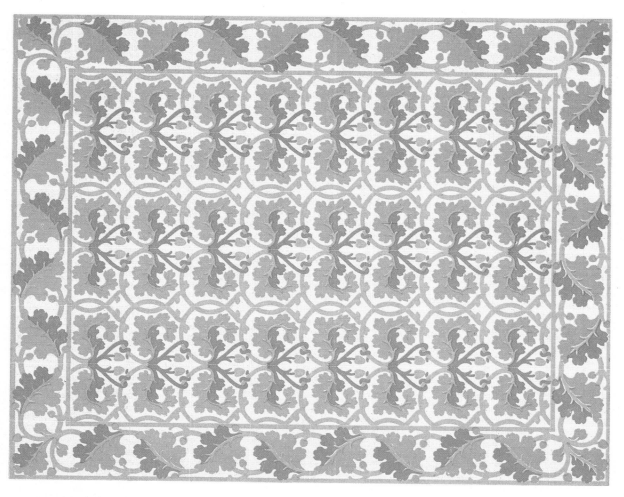

80

81

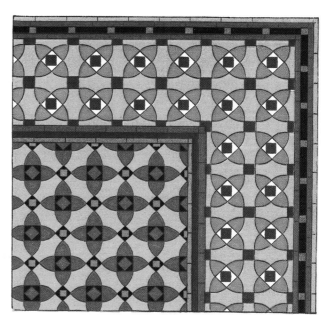
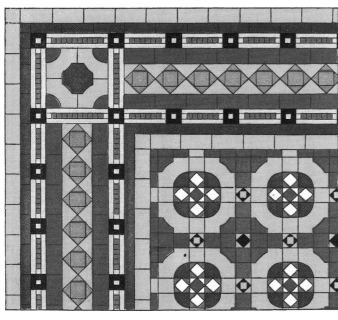

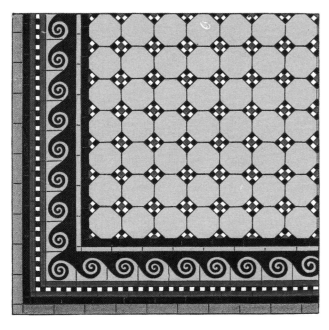

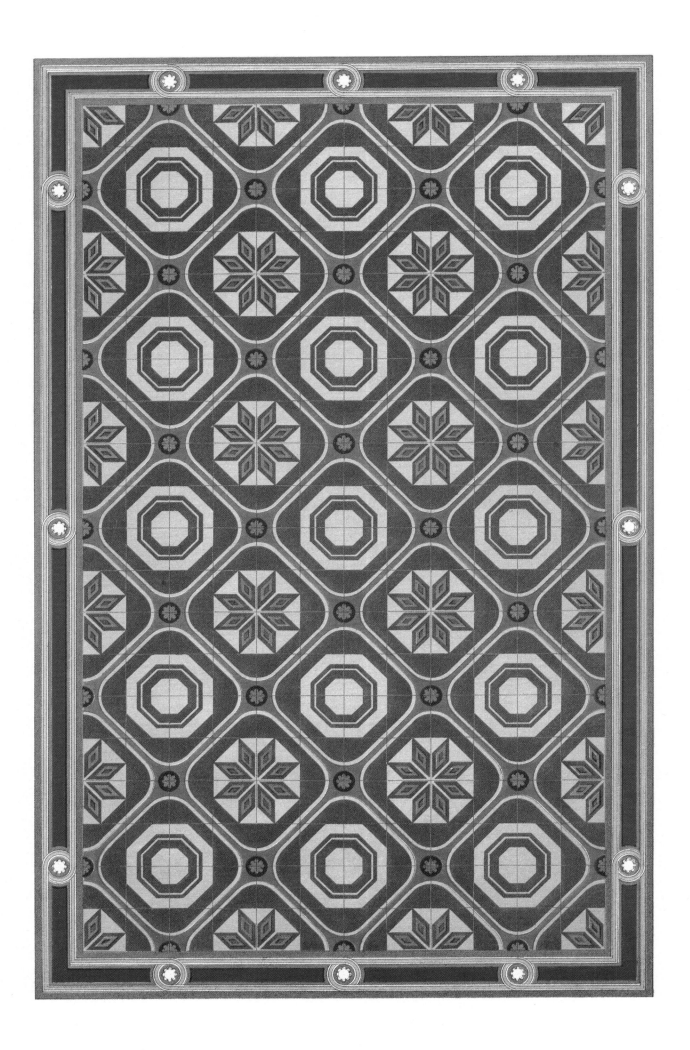

84

85

86

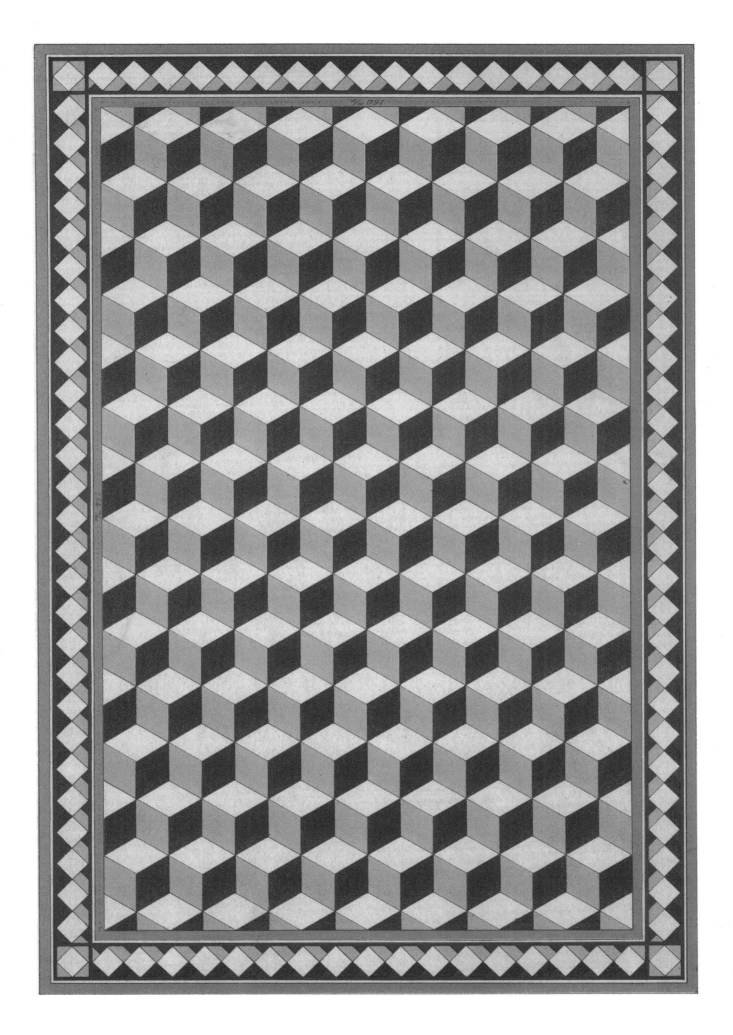

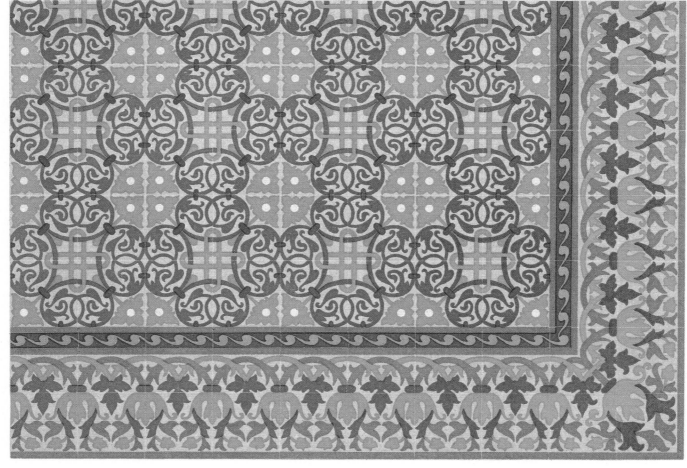

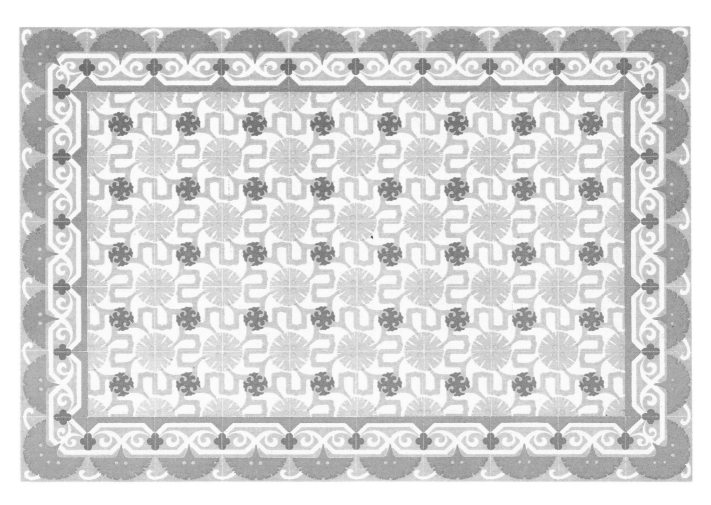

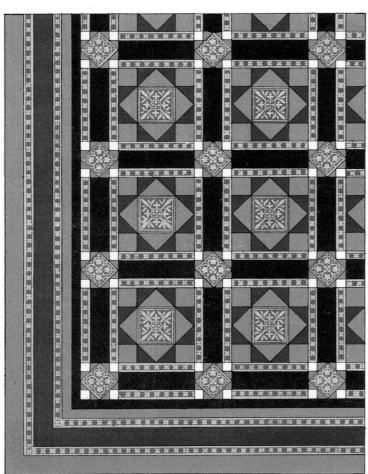